Trace the lower-case letters with your finger.

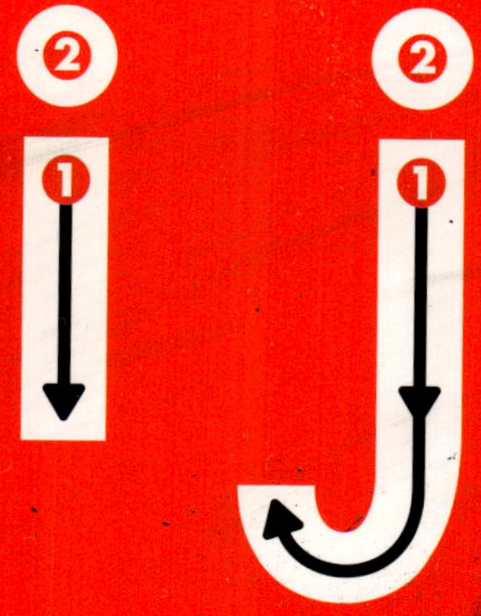

insect

jump

Follow the dashed lines from spaceship to alien.

Trace the letters.

Trace the lower-case letters with your finger.

Follow the dashed lines from goat to flower.

Trace the letters.

WIPE CLEAN
Age 3+

READY SET LEARN

Write Lower-case Letters

Wipe-clean practice in identifying and forming lower-case letters

r

rabbit

x

xylophone

a a a b b b c c c

Trace the lower-case letters with your finger.

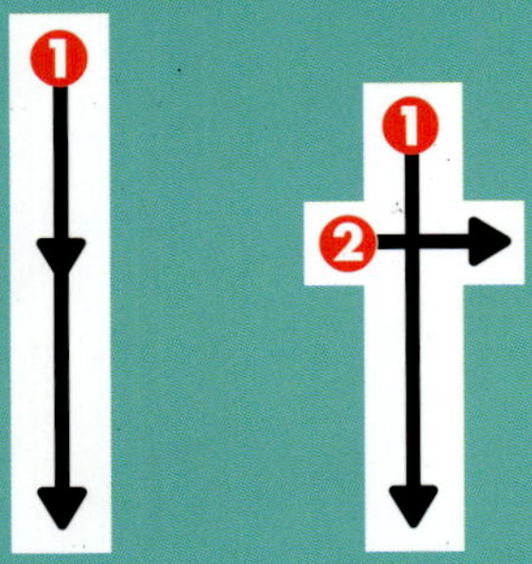

Follow the dashed lines from dog to bone.

Trace the letters.

Trace the lower-case letters with your finger.

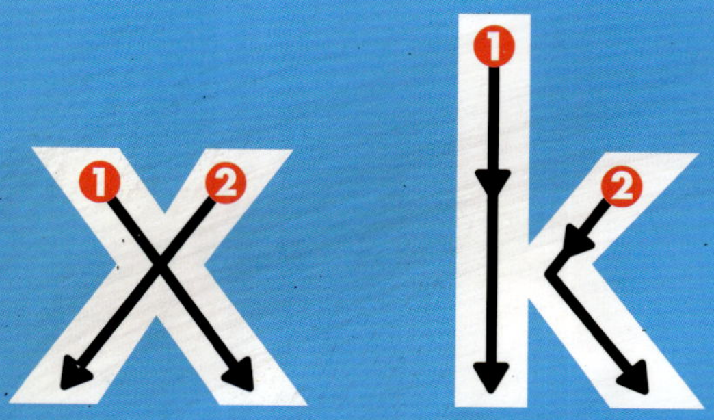

xylophone

kitten

Follow the dashed lines from cat to owner.

Trace the letters.

Trace the lower-case letters with your finger.

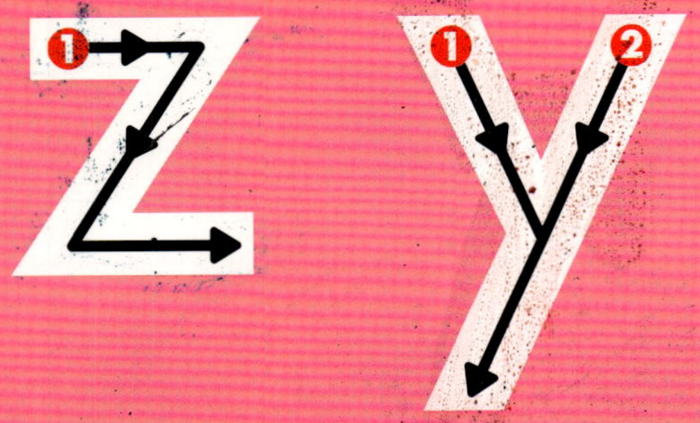

zebra

yacht

Follow the dashed lines from tractor to animal.

Trace the letters.

Trace the lower-case letters with your finger.

cat

egg

Follow the dashed lines from plane to island.

Trace the letters.

Trace the lower-case letters with your finger.

ambulance

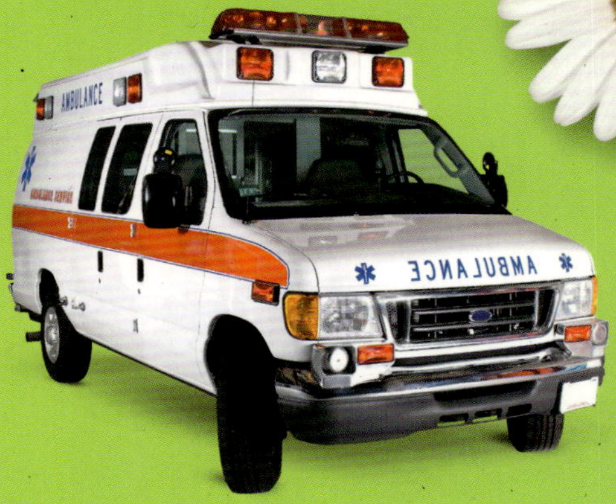

daisy

Follow the dashed lines from rabbit to burrow.

Trace the letters.

Trace the lower-case letters with your finger.

goat

quiet

Follow the dashed lines to make stalks and leaves.

Trace the letters.

Trace the lower-case letters with your finger.

unicycle

owl

Follow the dashed lines from fish to seaweed.

Trace the letters.

Trace the lower-case letters with your finger.

sock**s**

fish

Follow the dashed lines from bird to worm.

Trace the letters.

Trace the lower-case letters with your finger.

r p

rabbit

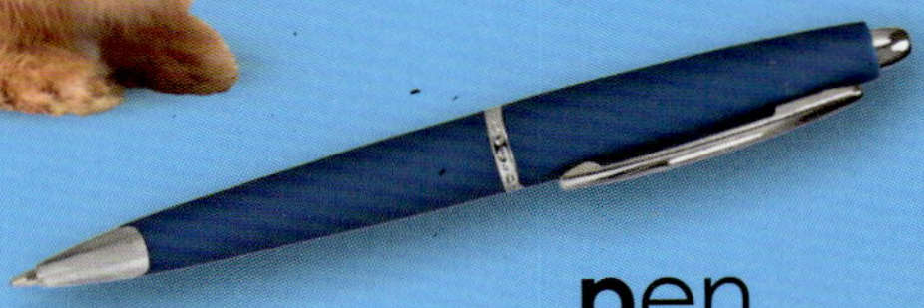

pen

Follow the dashed lines from rabbit to carrot.

Trace the letters.

r r r p p p

Trace the lower-case letters with your finger.

b h

house

boat

Follow the dashed lines down and around from mouse to cheese.

Trace the letters.

b b b h h h

Trace the lower-case letters with your finger.

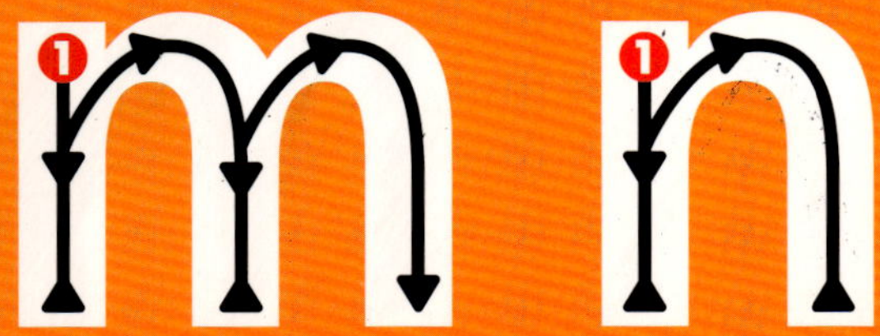

Follow the dashed lines from frog to fly.

Trace the letters.

Trace the alphabet.

a b c d

e f g h

i j k l m

n o p q

r s t u v

w x y z

READY SET LEARN

Write Lower-case Letters

The early years are an important period in children's learning and a vital stepping stone for their success in school. This wipe-clean workbook provides teacher-approved activities to help children in important curriculum areas. The wipe-clean pages mean children can practise again and again, and build confidence while they learn.

Introducing the letters in an order that keeps like-shapes together, this book focuses on:

Pre-writing activities involving practising the shapes needed to form lower-case letters

•

Learning the letter shapes by tracing them with a finger

•

Practising the letters by tracing them with a wipe-clean pen

Promotes hand-eye coordination

Tracing and writing activities help develop children's hand-eye coordination.

Promotes writing skills

Give children plenty of practice in forming letters. Wipe the pages clean and allow children to repeat them until they are confident.

Stimulates adult-child interaction

Talk to children about what they are doing. Assisting them in the early stages helps them to learn more quickly and gain in confidence.

make believe ideas ltd
The Wilderness, Berkhamsted, Hertfordshire, HP4 2AZ, UK.

Recommended for children aged 3 years and over.
Manufactured in China. 04201801
www.makebelieveideas.com

Please retain this information for future reference
WARNING: SMALL PARTS NOT SUITABLE FOR CHILDREN UNDER 3 YEARS OF AGE - CHOKING HAZARD

£4.99

ISBN10: 1-78843-352-1
ISBN13: 978-1-78843-352-5
9 781788 433525

Conforms to Safety Standards AS/NZS ISO 8124